STAMP OUT
MAD

Edited by
Albert B. Feldstein

WARNER BOOKS

A Warner Communications Company

WARNER BOOKS EDITION

Copyright © 1977, 1978 and 1984 by E.C. Publications, Inc.
All rights reserved. No part of this book may be reproduced
without permission. For information address:
E.C. Publications, Inc.
485 Madison Avenue
New York, N.Y. 10022

Title "MAD" used with permission of its owner,
E.C. Publications, Inc.

This Warner Books Edition is published by
arrangement with E.C. Publications, Inc.

Designed by Thomas Nozkowski

Warner Books, Inc.
666 Fifth Avenue
New York, N.Y. 10103

 A Warner Communications Company

Printed in the United States of America

First Printing: June, 1984

Reissued: April 1, 1990

10 9 8 7 6 5 4 3 2

ATTENTION SCHOOLS

WARNER books are available at quantity discounts with bulk
purchase for educational use. For information, please write to:
SPECIAL SALES DEPARTMENT, WARNER BOOKS, 666 FIFTH
AVENUE, NEW YORK, NY 10103.

IT'S STALLONE RANGER! DEPT.

For years, Hollywood made movies about the Fight Game that were loaded with clichés. Recently, however, instead of bringing back another one of those "Joe Palooka" pictures, they made a brand new type movie about the Fight Game... loaded with brand new clichés. You'll see what we mean in this version of

ROCK-HEAD

ARTIST: MORT DRUCKER   WRITER: STAN HART

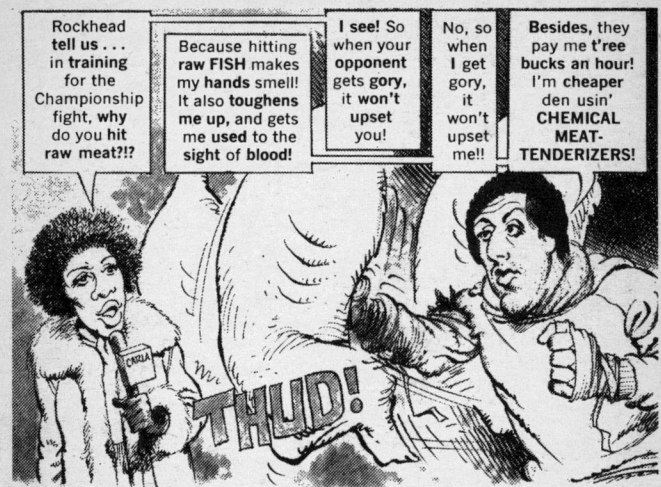

DON MARTIN DEPT.

ONE EVENING IN A BUS STATION

BERG'S-EYE VIEW DEPT.

THE LIGHTER SIDE OF...

SUMMER PROBLEMS

ARTIST & WRITER:
DAVID BERG

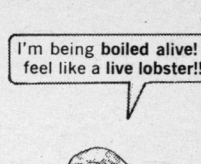

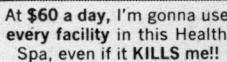

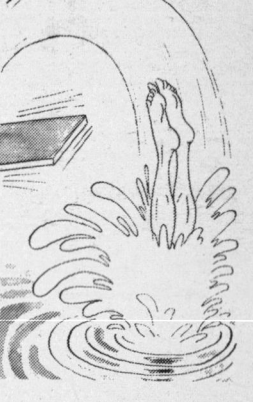

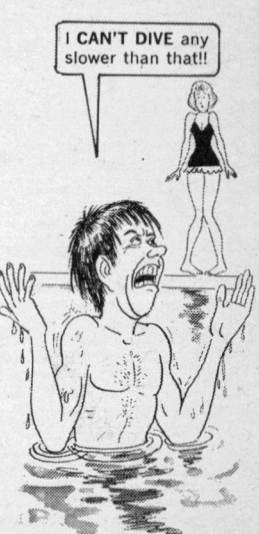

JOKE AND DAGGER DEPT.

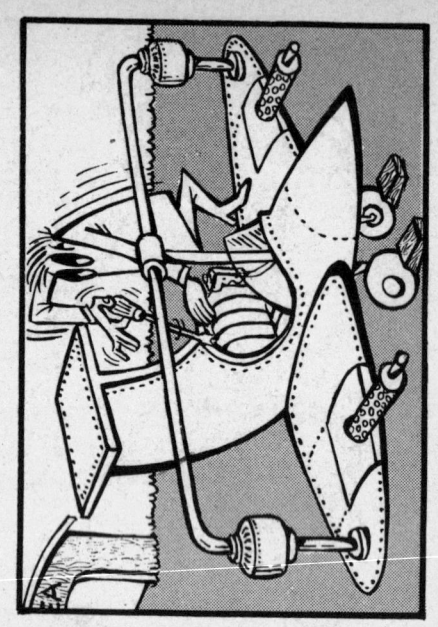

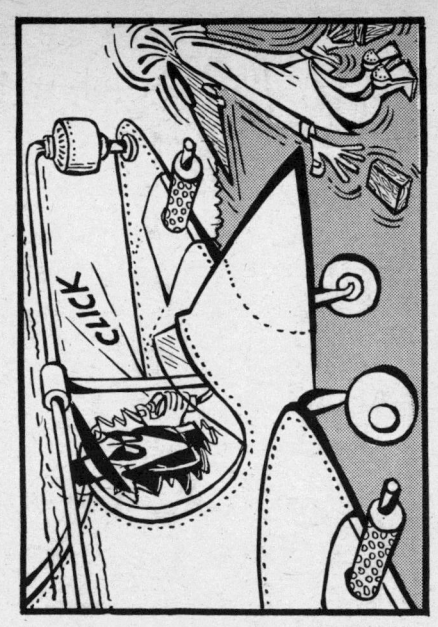
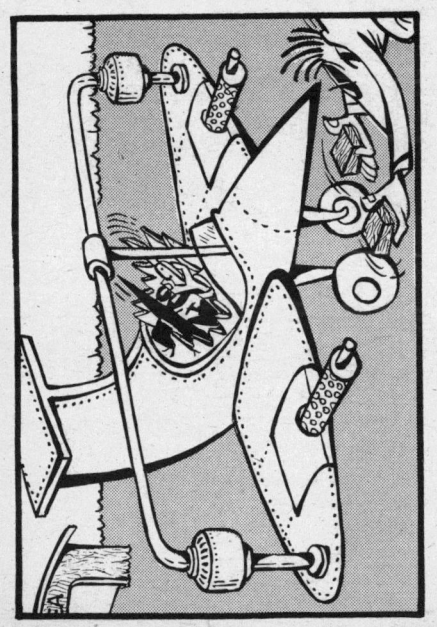

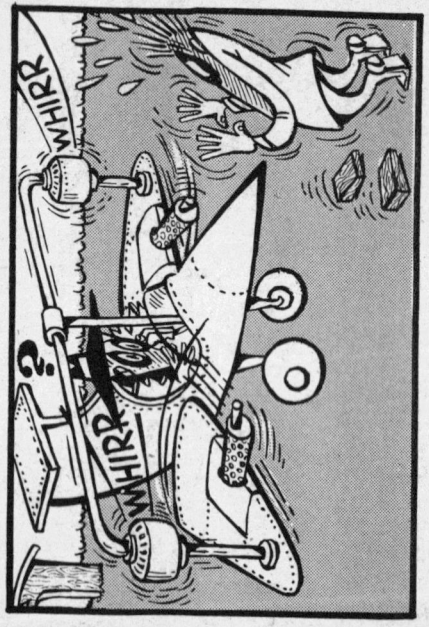

BENT OFFERINGS DEPT.

SOME LEGENDARY WIRE HANGERS

ARTIST: BOB CLARKE
WRITER: PAUL PETER PORGES

ZORRO'S WIRE HANGER

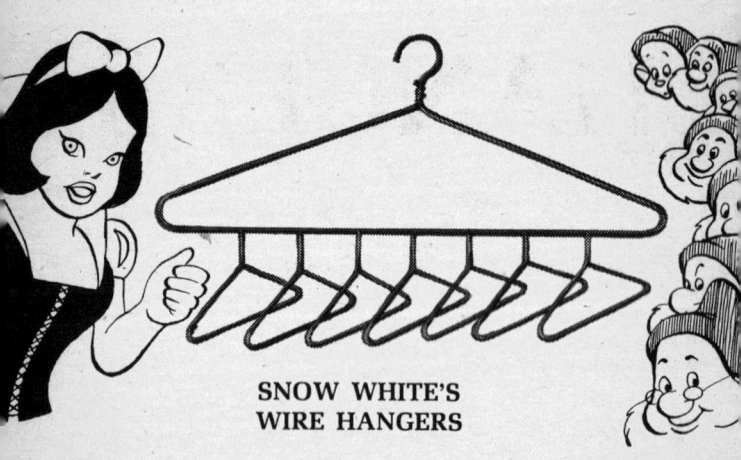

SNOW WHITE'S WIRE HANGERS

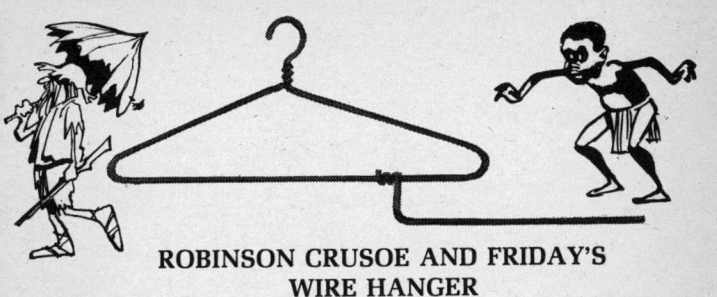

ROBINSON CRUSOE AND FRIDAY'S WIRE HANGER

TOULOUSE-LAUTREC'S WIRE HANGER

THE HUNCHBACK OF NOTRE DAME'S WIRE HANGER

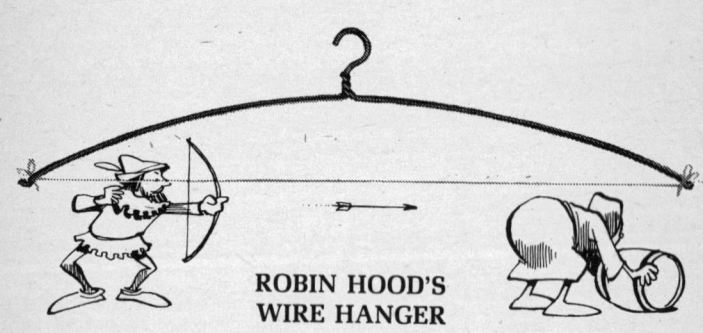

ROBIN HOOD'S WIRE HANGER

THE FRANKENSTEIN MONSTER'S WIRE HANGER

DR. JEKYLL AND MR. HYDE'S WIRE HANGER

THE ROTO-ROOTER MAN'S WIRE HANGER

LADY GODIVA'S WIRE HANGER

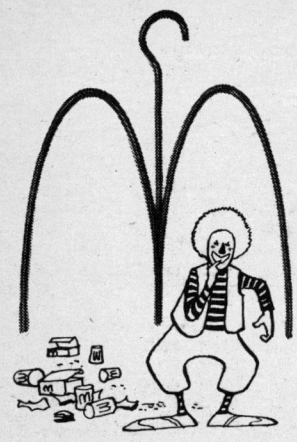

RONALD McDONALD'S WIRE HANGER

ALFRED E. NEUMAN'S WIRE HANGER

PUT YOUR FUNNY WHERE YOUR MOUTH IS DEPT.

NOTE: A number of years ago, we ran a few articles entitled "MAD's Cliché Killers." Perhaps most of you were too young (or too smart) to read them, so we'll go over the premise again. But pay attention, it may be the last time!

PREMISE OF ARTICLE: Ahem! Have you noticed that most people talk in clichés? The worst part of a cliché is

MAD'S CLICHÉ

COMING HOME LATE

that it's not really conversation, since a cliché doesn't require an answer. What are you supposed to say when those morons ask, "Hot enough for you?" Are they really looking for a response? Of course not! But now you can surprise them! Because here is some ammunition to fire right back at those insufferable cliché poppers. We call them...

KILLERS

ARTIST: PAUL COKER, JR.
WRITER: STAN HART

VISITING A DOCTOR'S OFFICE

WORKING ON A JOB

SHOPPING IN A DEPARTMENT STORE

PLAYING IN LITTLE LEAGUE

GETTING ARRESTED

CODE FRONT MOVING IN DEPT.

Perhaps you've noticed that more and more groceries and magazines we buy these days are imprinted with this ugly little example of "op-art". Well, this is the "UNIVERSAL PRODUCTS CODE" symbol. It was designed to enable computers to ring up the prices on your purchase. Someday, the "UPC" symbol will eliminate surly cashiers who take forever, make mistakes and bruise the lettuce! Yep, they'll be replaced by surly machines that take forever, make mistakes and bruise the lettuce. That's progress! And that'll only be the beginning. Here's what we'll see...

WHEN THE SYMBOL

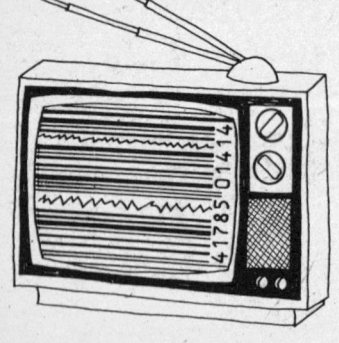

"UPC" TAKES OVER COMPLETELY

ARTIST & WRITER: HENRY CLARK

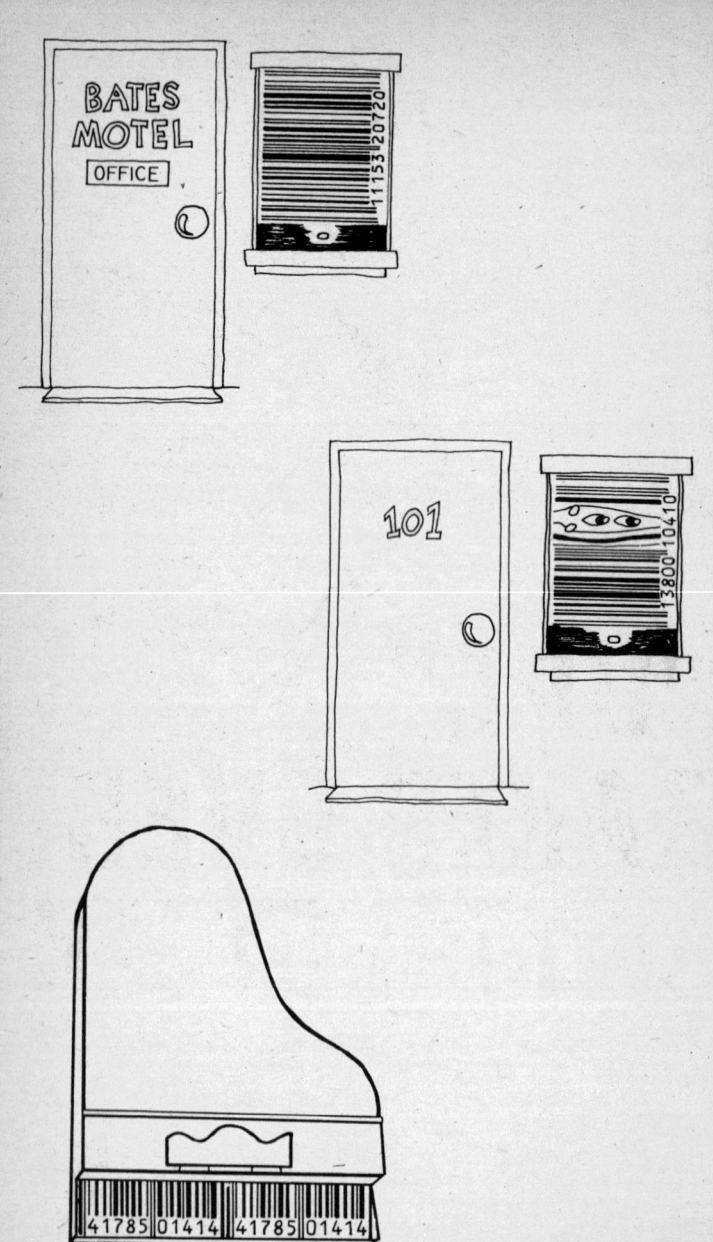

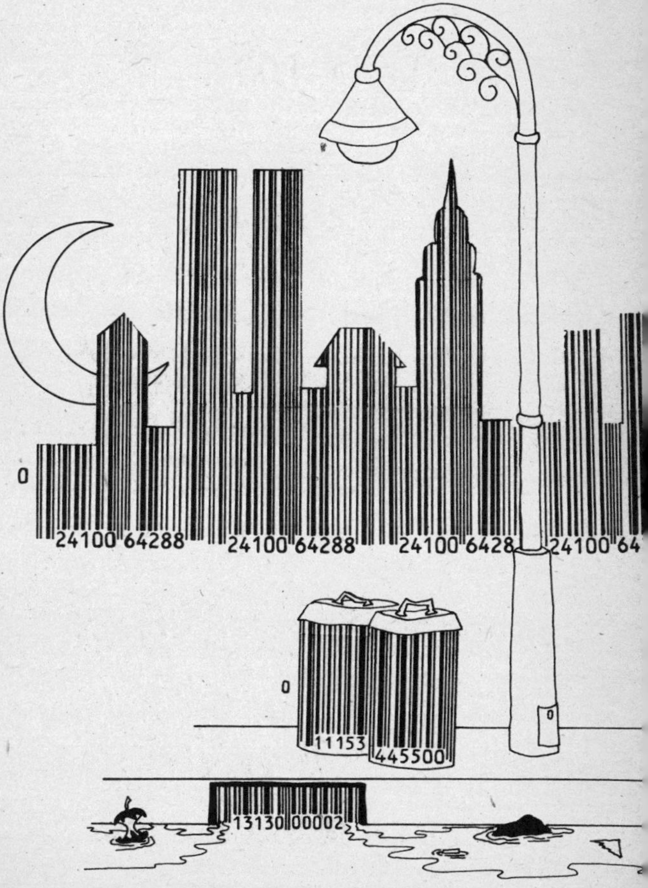

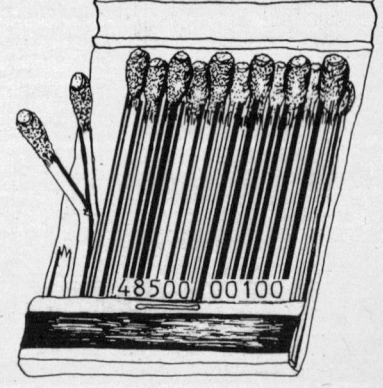

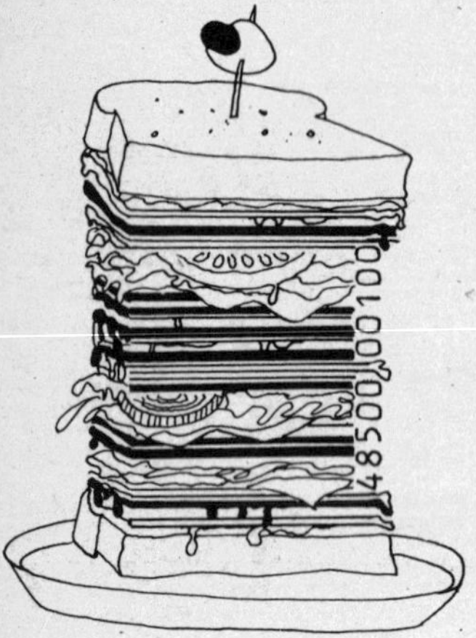

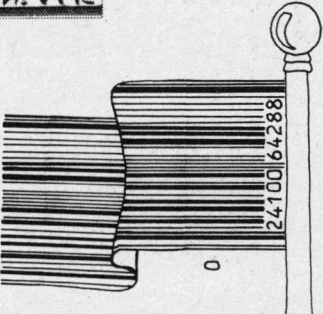

DON MARTIN DEPT.

ONE MORNING IN A PRISON TOWER

LAPPING IT UP DEPT.

MAD GOES TO A BUFFET SUPPER

ARTIST & WRITER: PAUL PETER PORGES

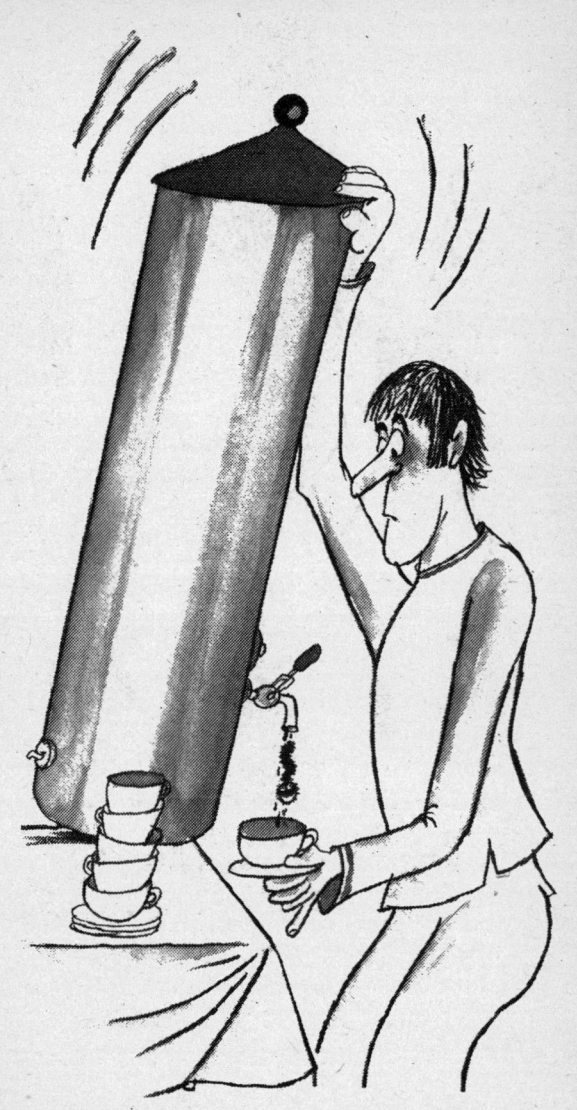

DON MARTIN DEPT.

EARLY ONE MORNING OUT ON THE BAY

CLASS STRUGGLE DEPT.

A MAD LOOK AT A MODERN HIGH SCHOOL

ARTIST: JACK DAVIS   WRITER: LOU SILVERSTONE

TRIED AND TRUDEAU DEPT.

There's a new look to the comics, and the man most responsible for it is Gary Trudeau, the creator of "Doonesbury". Thanks to Gary, more and more strips are becoming intellectual and cerebral and involved

in the social issues of today. The old strips, however, stay the same as they were—with the same stock situations and routines. Eventually, they'll have to get with it, and we'll see what happens...

...When Those "Old Line" Comic Strips Follow The New Wave, Cerebral "Doonesbury" Trend

ARTIST: JACK RICKARD
WRITER: FRANK JACOBS

DICK TRACY

LI'L ABNER

SCHLOCK 'N' ROLL DEPT.

Hi! I'm Anita Tyrant! You remember me and my famous battle cry? "Oranges, Si! Rotten fruits, No!" Anyway, I'm with you this issue to explore a truly unique phenomenon on today's music scene! Namely, **"Punk Rock"**! And in a little while, you're going to meet

MAD'S "PUNK ROCK GROUP" OF THE YEAR

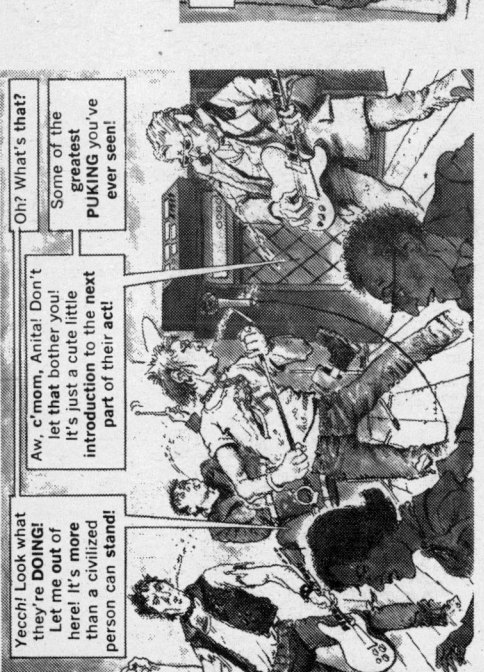

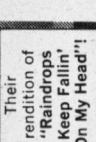
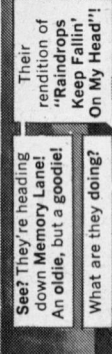

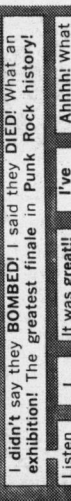

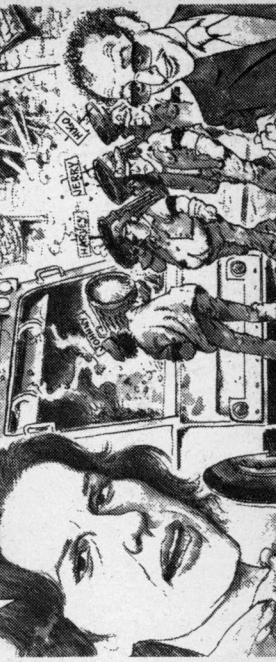

TWIN SCREWS DEPT.

"Catch-22" was a best-selling book that later was made into a successful movie. In case you didn't read the book or see the movie, it was about an Air Force bombardier who doesn't want to fly any more dangerous missions. Since there is an Air Force regulation which states that if you're insane, you can't fly, our hero tells his

MAD'S

Your Dad says you can stay out as late as you want on weekends if you get straight A's . . .

shrink that he's crazy and therefore, according to regulations, he doesn't have to fly. But there's a catch—Catch-22—which states that if you don't want to fly dangerous missions, it proves you're sane . . . and therefore, you have to keep flying! All of which is our roundabout way of introducing . . .

REAL-LIFE "CATCH-22's"

. . . but if you get straight A's, none of the guys will ask you out because you're obviously a brain.

ARTIST: SERGIO ARAGONES
WRITER: LOU SILVERSTONE

You can't watch TV until you finish all your homework...

...but by the time you finish all your homework, your favorite shows are over.

You're given permission to have the gang over for a party, but you're not allowed to have beer ...

... and if there's no beer, the gang won't come to your party.

If you're over 12, you have to pay an adult admission price at the movies...

...but because you're under 18, you're only allowed to see boring "kid" movies.

That great-looking cheerleader won't go out with you unless you're on the football team...

...but if you make the team, you have an early curfew, and she won't go out with guys who have to sign in at 11:00 o'clock.

You're threatened with Summer School if you don't pass all your subjects...

... but if you do pass, you'll have to go to Summer Camp ... which is worse.

You have one of those cool teachers who doesn't take attendance, and doesn't care if you show up for his lectures or not . . .

. . . but if he springs a surprise quiz on the class, and you're not there . . . you get a big fat zero.

Your favorite team signs several free agents for a couple of million bucks...

...but in order to pay for them, they raise the ticket prices, so now you can't afford to see your favorite team play.

If you want dessert, you have to finish your broccoli first...

... but if you eat all your broccoli, you're sure to barf, and you won't want any dessert.

WHAT'S IN AN AIM? DEPT.

It's not easy making big decisions. Some people flip a coin. Other people consult the I Ching. There are even a few idiots who ask for the advice of experts, weigh merits and look into their own experience. Today the "In" method is throwing darts at a dartboard. Where the dart lands tells

DECISION-

WARREN BEATTY

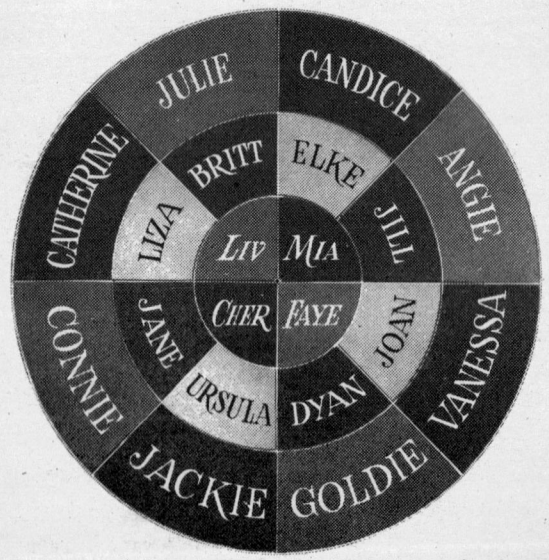

the person whether or not he should buy a new car, or carry out the garbage, or finish reading this ridiculous, time wasting article. Celebrities are no different. They, too, have their important decisions to make, and to help them in their hour of need we now present these

MAKING DART BOARDS

FOR CELEBRITIES

ARTIST: BOB CLARKE
WRITERS: FRANK JACOBS
AND WILLIAM MCCOLE

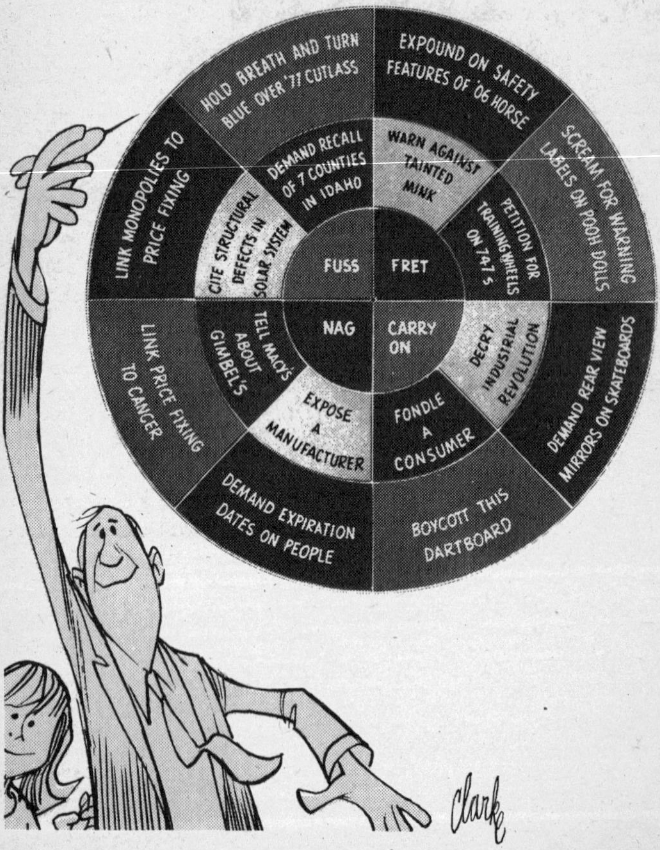

CHARLES BRONSON

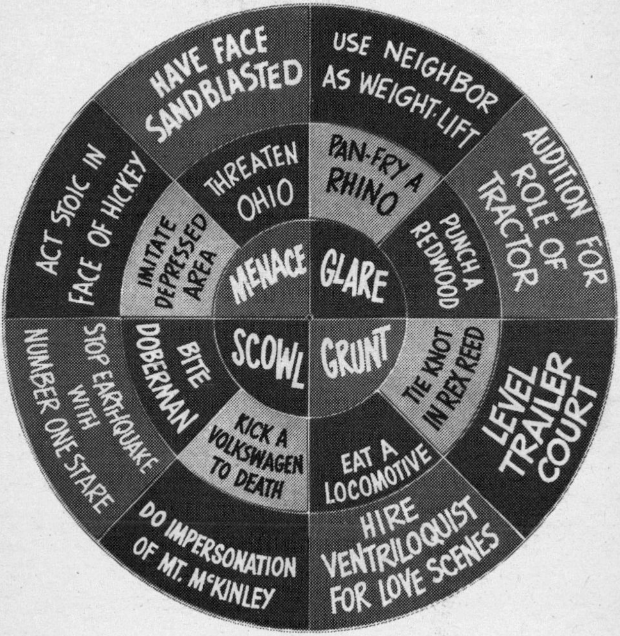

Wheel sections (outer ring, clockwise):
- HAVE FACE SANDBLASTED
- USE NEIGHBOR AS WEIGHT-LIFT
- AUDITION FOR ROLE OF TRACTOR
- LEVEL TRAILER COURT
- HIRE VENTRILOQUIST FOR LOVE SCENES
- DO IMPERSONATION OF MT. McKINLEY
- STOP EARTHQUAKE WITH NUMBER ONE STARE
- ACT STOIC IN FACE OF HICKEY

Middle ring:
- THREATEN OHIO
- PAN-FRY A RHINO
- PUNCH A REDWOOD
- TIE THE KNOT IN REX REED
- EAT A LOCOMOTIVE
- KICK A VOLKSWAGEN TO DEATH
- BITE DOBERMAN
- IMITATE DEPRESSED AREA

Inner ring:
- MENACE
- GLARE
- GRUNT
- SCOWL

FARRAH FAWCETT-MAJORS

EVEL KNIEVEL

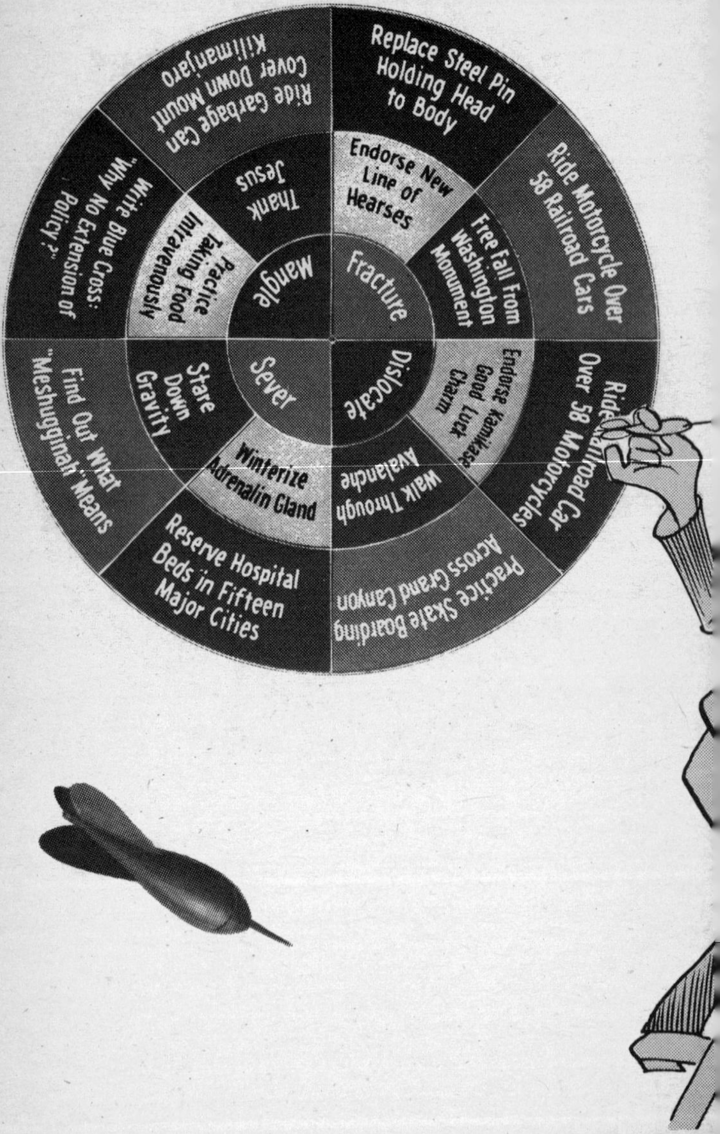

BILLY GRAHAM

ILIE NASTASE

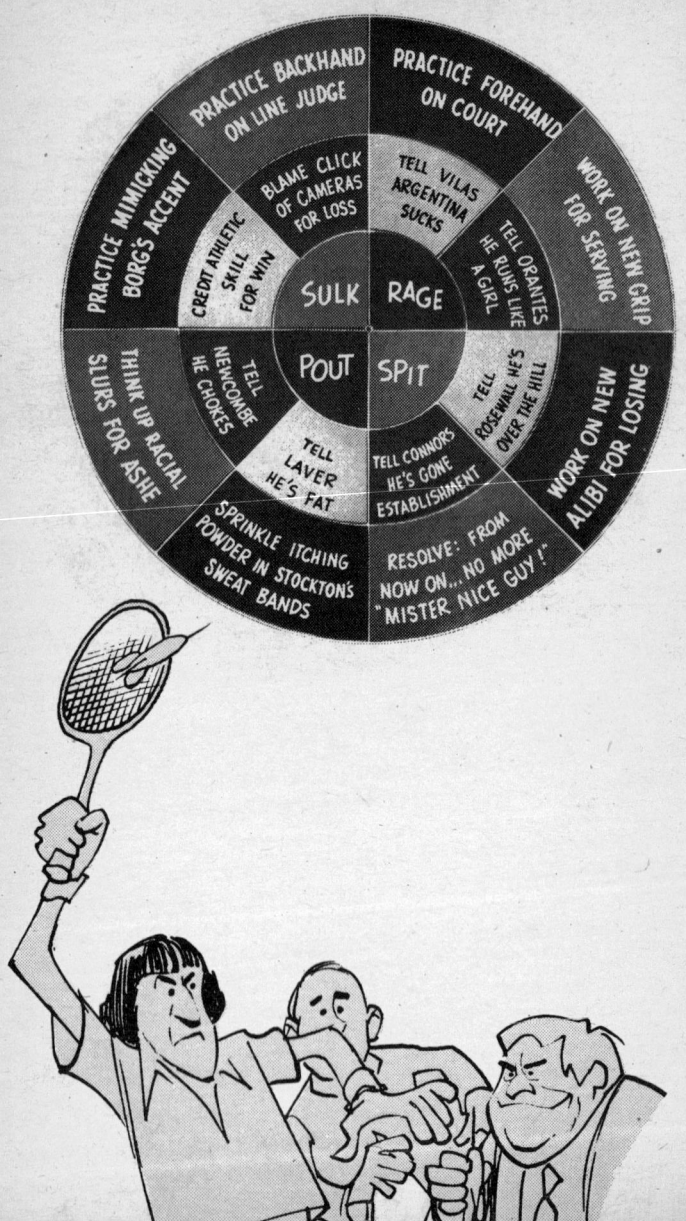

ANN LANDERS

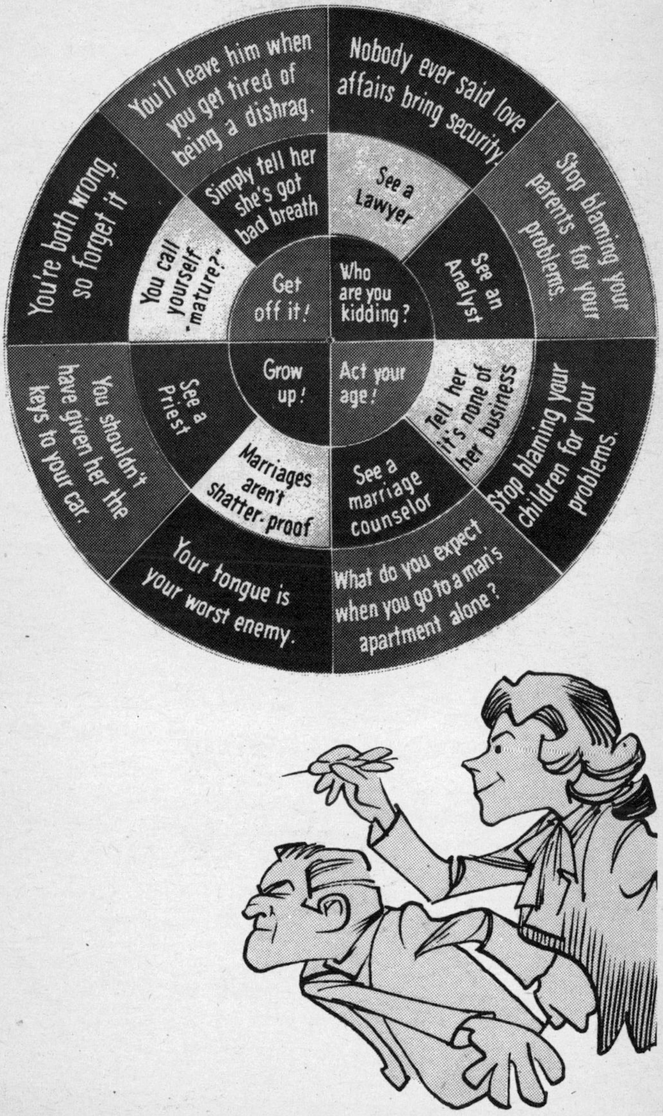

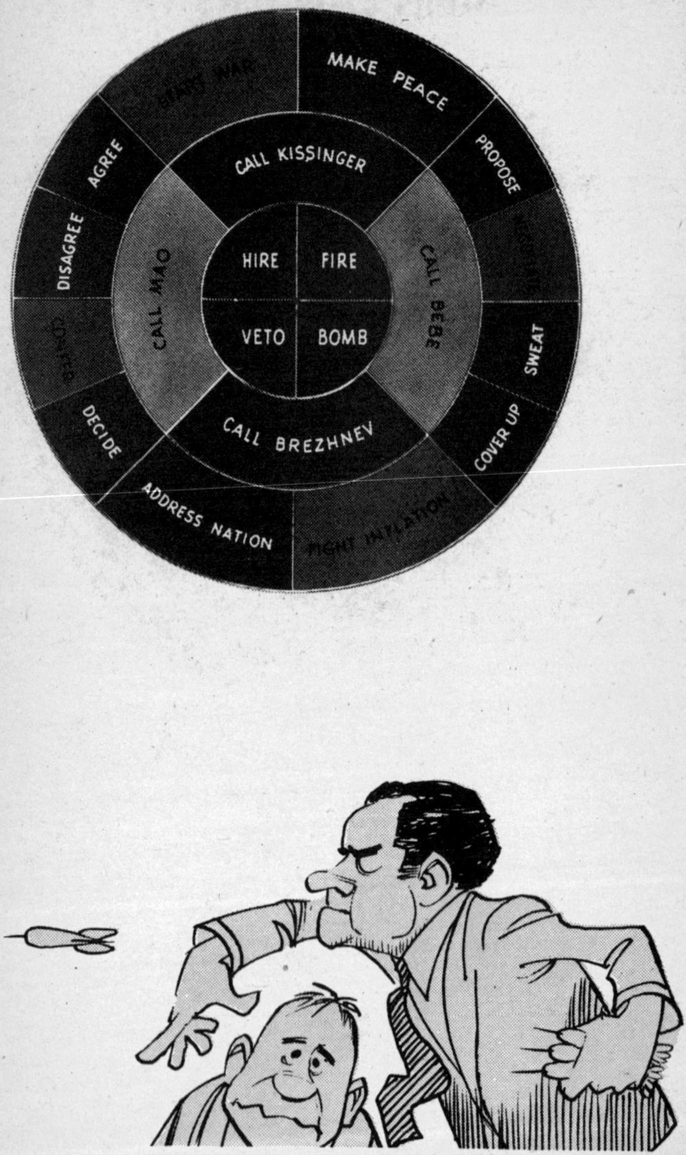

EX-PRESIDENT NIXON

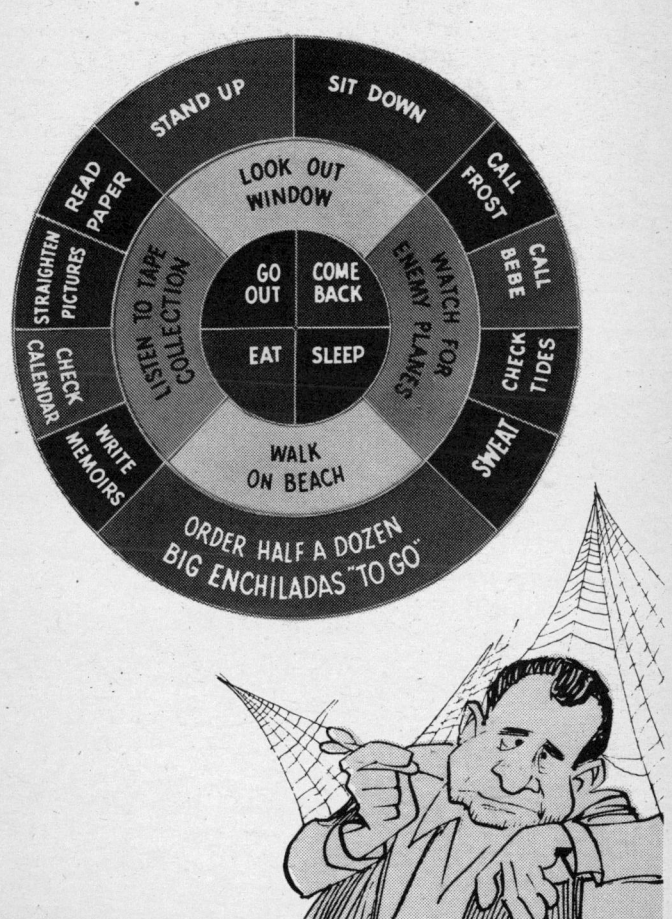

WILLIAM F. BUCKLEY JR.

MUHAMMAD ALI

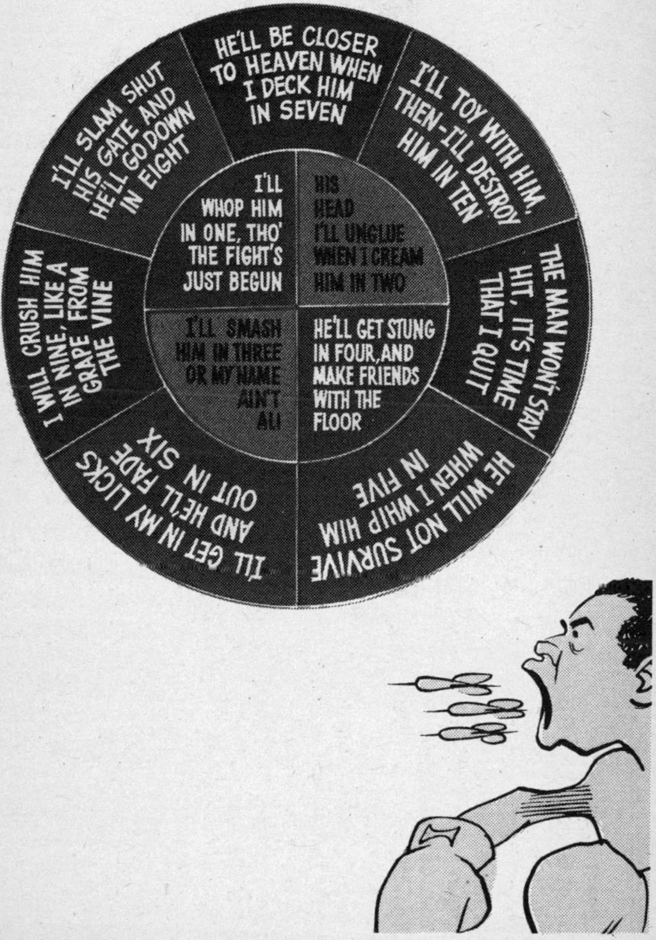

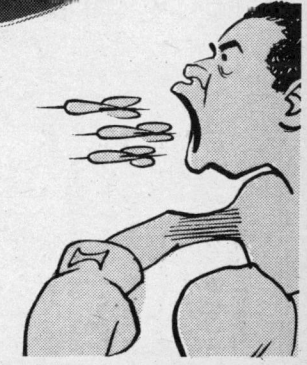

AWFUL ASSEMBLY DEPT.

GRADUATING CLASS PICTURES

Like this example most Graduating Class pictures are usually unexciting groupings of the subjects, lacking in creativity and void of inspiration. Which got us at MAD to thinking that it really doesn't have to be that way. Like f'rinstance, why not hire talented people to stage interesting interpretations of these usually deadly groupings? Like these

AS STAGED BY

SOME OF THE WORLD'S BEST-KNOWN PICTURE-MAKERS

BUSBY BERKELEY · CECIL B. De MILLE · JOHN FORD · FEDERICO FELLINI · ALFRED HITCHCOCK · SAM PECKINPAH · MEL BROOKS · WOODY ALLEN · STEVEN SPIELBERG

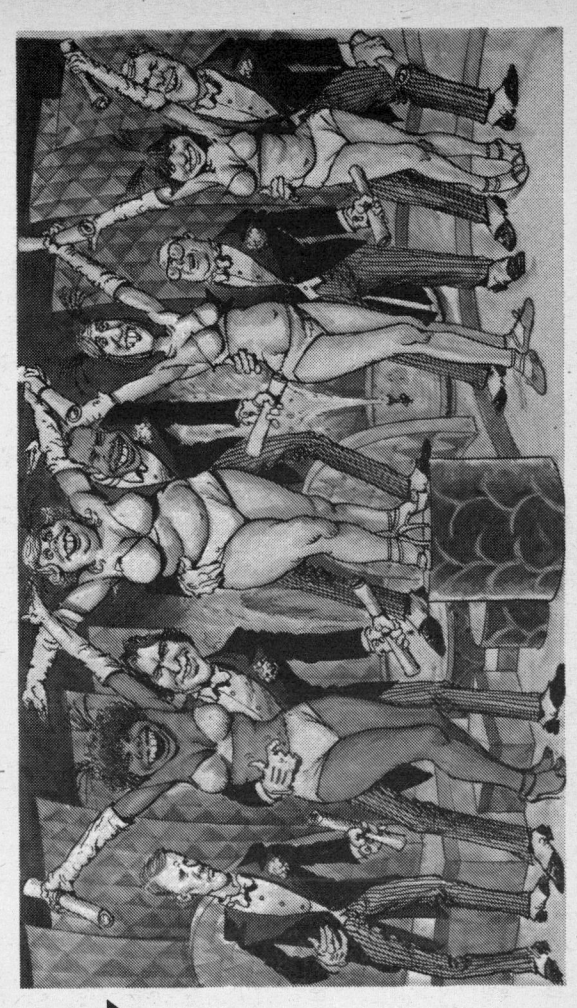

BUSBY BERKELEY

CECIL B. DE MILLE

JOHN FORD

FEDERICO FELLINI

ALFRED HITCHCOCK

MEL BROOKS

SAM PECKINPAH

WOODY ALLEN

STEVEN SPIELBERG

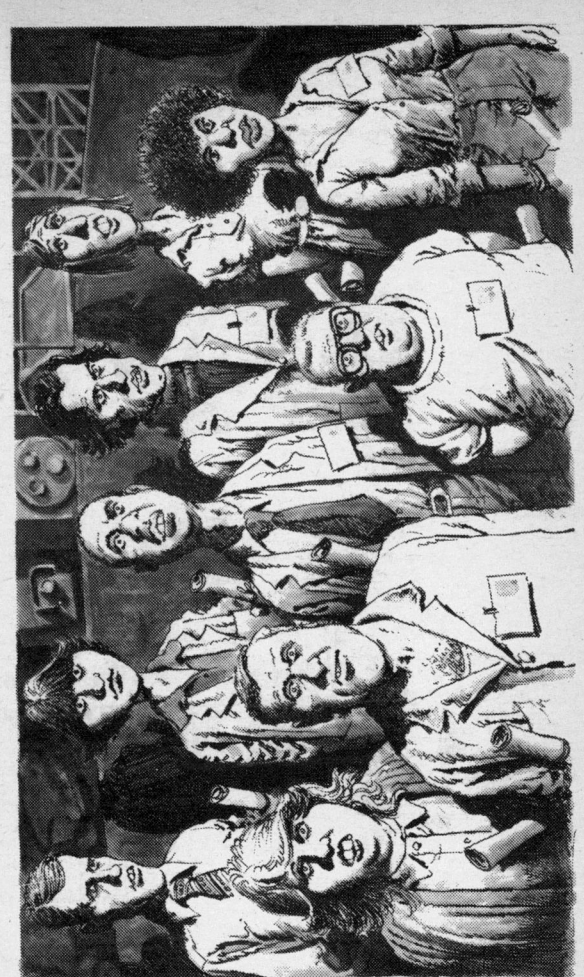

BERG'S-EYE VIEW DEPT.

THE LIGHTER SIDE OF...

WA

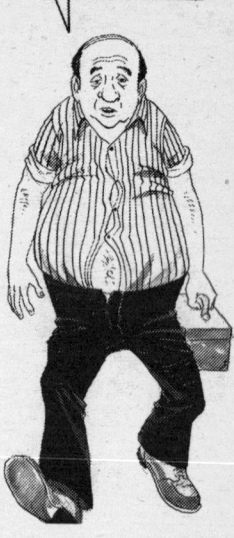

HEXERCISE DEPT.

STAY IN S

YOU START LIFTING WEIGHTS

Each and every muscle in your body is specially toned and developed by its very own specific weight exercise...

ING
HAPE

...and then, one evening, you crash through your weakened floor boards... and you break every bone in your body.

WRITER & ARTIST:
DEAN NORMAN

YOU EAT ONLY ORGANIC FOODS

The natural, pure nutrients present in organically-grown foods promise to increase your lifespan by twenty years...

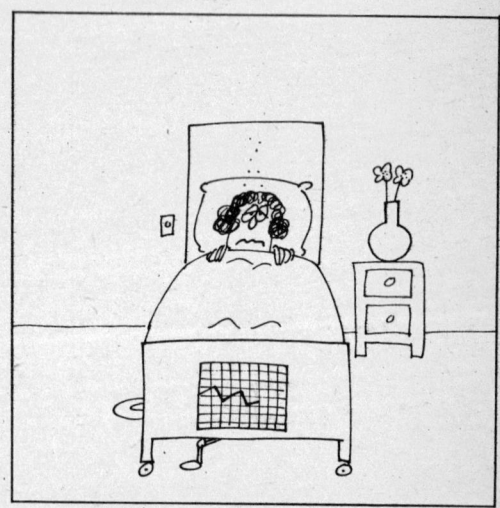

...and then the brand of organically-grown mushrooms you've been eating is suddenly recalled because of botulism.

YOU QUIT DRINKING

Your nerves are steady, your head is clear, your boss promotes you, your wife and children love you again...

...and then you get punched out by an angry drunk who can't stand your righteous "holier-than-thou" attitude.

YOU QUIT SMOKING

Your appetite improves as you start deep-breathing fresh air again...

...and then you develop emphysema from deep-breathing fresh smoggy air.

YOU TAKE UP BICYCLING

Your daily grueling rides build up tremendous strength in your legs...

...and then, one morning, a pack of wild dogs almost chews your legs off.

YOU TAKE UP JOGGING

The early morning workouts start to build up your vigor and stamina...

...until the morning you finally can cross the park...and you're mugged.

YOU TAKE UP BACKPACKING

It's back to nature, exercising in a clean and beautiful environment...

...until the weekend you get lost in the woods and nearly starve to death.

YOU TAKE UP CANOEING

Paddling peacefully across a sylvan lake not only builds up your body, but also gives you peace of mind...

...until, one day, you're run down by some idiot in a water-ski tow-boat.

DON MARTIN DEPT.

ONE
AFTERNOON
IN
DOWNTOWN
LOURDES

SWITCH HIT DEPT.

HE'S COMPANY

ARTIST: ANGELO TORRES WRITER: ARNIE KOGEN

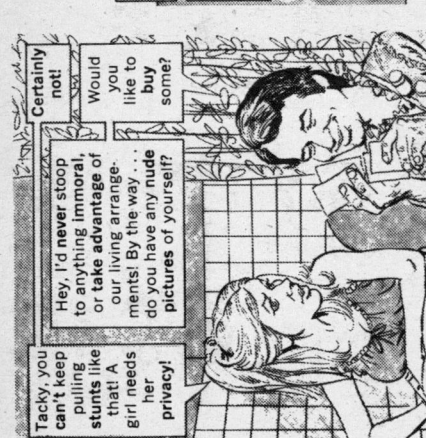